LITTLE KNOWN FACTS ABOUT BUNDLING IN THE NEW WORLD

The Old-Fashioned Custom of Lovers or Travelers Sleeping in the Same Bed, Usually Without the Formality of Undressing

By A. MONROE AURAND, Jr.
Member: Penna.-German Society,
Huguenot Society of Penna., &c.

The Bundling Bag
A mighty convenient arrangement for man and maid—and practical, too—just so long as the girl kept both her feet enclosed!

WILDSIDE PRESS

PERTINENT!

THE men in the shops, in the fields, in the offices; the professional men and the tots in school, ought to, and must be made more fully acquainted with their coming into the community through a generous and right-thinking ancestry; and there is no more profitable, agreeable and consistent way in which this education of the people can be accomplished, than through an applied study and reading of such books as local history, in all the schools and homes of the country. If the achievements of those of the pioneer days are not worthy of mention and study at this day and age, of how much less value and appreciation will our labors appear to those of a not-far-off-tomorrow?

PREFACE

THIS is the author's fifth title on the subject of "bundling." We all hope it will be his last—but he reserves the right to issue another, perhaps larger, comprehensive title later.

It is not always the student of history who makes known some of the interesting facts of passing time—but he can use his good offices to collate and bring these incidents to their proper place in history. That is what we are doing, and from time to time there will issue from this same source items on various subjects, sometimes more or less old, but obtained by original research and from those who have taken part in the drama of life.

The author is not particularly interested in the subject of "bundling," personally, except as a guide to the passing of time; no more interested in "pow-wowing" than the average physician—but enough to bring to light whatever there is available on this subject, particularly with respect to its practice in the state of Pennsylvania.

We have had testimonials almost without number concerning the value of such social studies as we already have presented. Dr. Brooks, late of the Department of Sociology, Univ. of North Carolina, says: "While there is considerable general material on the custom of bundling we feel that yours has a certain authenticity and interest which are unique."

Dr. Otto L. Schmidt, prominent Chicagoan, active historian, public-spirited-citizen, now deceased, said: "Congratulations to you as an entertainer of our people through good literature, with valuable information."

Walter C. Brenner, Esq., of Philadelphia, in a limited edition of only five copies on "Bundling," states: "Aurand in recent times has done excellent research work . . . and gives a good view of this custom among the Penna.-Germans."

Dana Doten, in "The Art of Bundling," says: In recent times Pennsylvania has taken the lead in bundling. And there the situation is rather complicated. The chief authority . . . is A. Monroe Aurand, Jr. . . ."

In some twenty titles in the past ten years, we have covered a gap in the history of this great state, which, if left to others more capable, might easily have been lost in time to come.

The history of the state, or nation, is that of the experience of all her citizens, of all time, whether in bed, or on the woodbox; whether in farming or industrial life; whether in the pulpit or on the stages of our little community theatres.

Readers are invited to send to the author all references to "bundling," whether in their community, or elsewhere—original or otherwise—with a view to using same in later editions.

A. M. A., Jr.

Harrisburg, Pa.

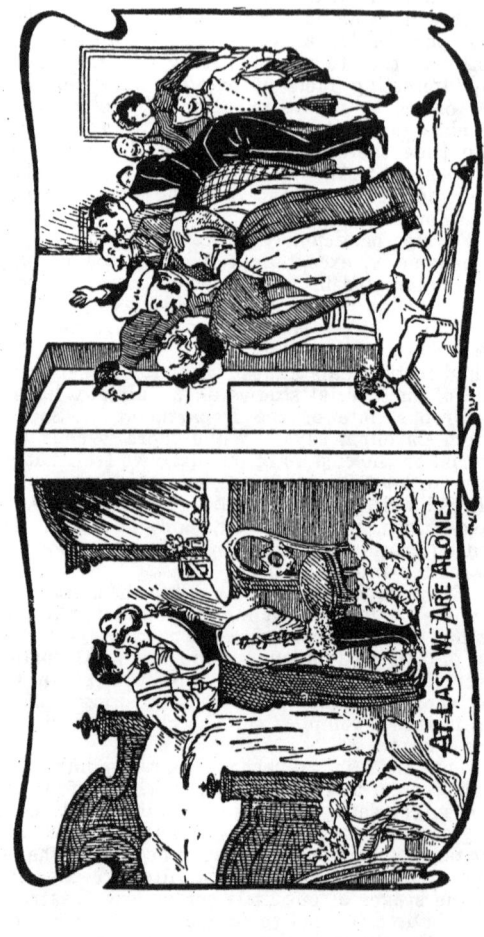

A "professional bundler," perhaps, at a hotel! How truly typical of the couple on the left, "all alone" with their thoughts—and the "spectators" on the right

WHAT IDEAS DO YOU HOLD RELATIVE TO COURTING IN BED?

CAN LOVERS GO TO BED, SAFELY, WHILE WEARING THEIR CLOTHES, AND STILL BE CHASTE? Is it morally wrong for one to go to bed to court—and morally right to sit up all night for the same purpose?

The natural love of man for woman, and woman for man, and the almost universal lack of knowledge regarding the widespread custom of clothed, or partly clothed persons

B U N D L I N G — (or courting in bed)

induces us to publish another of our historical accounts for real lovers of folk-lore.

Let-yourself-go for an hour or so, and catch-up with your grand-fathers and grand-mothers in Pennsylvania, and in New England. But don't forget that "bundling," or "tarrying," was also practiced in the British Isles, and the continent of Europe, as well as in the Far East and Near East.

The dictionaries define the term:

"BUNDLE (bundled, bundling). To occupy the same bed without undressing;—said of a man and woman, especially during courtship."—(See "Webster's Collegiate Dictionary," 1938, et. al.)

These accounts have been obtained largely from original sources—from men and women who have bundled, and who were never sorry that they did.

Many declared that it was the means of bringing them into close harmony with chaste young women, eventually ending in a happy and fruitful marriage.

If there is anything that "makes" a man want to be friendly with the rest of the world, it is when he sees an innocent young couple engaged in the hand-in-hand type of courtship.

This feeling is even increased when we see what transpires on the park benches, and in the parks, on the porch-swings, and in the automobile; even the theatre balcony, or dark recesses, reveal the emotion of lovers; the decks of ferry-boats and the corridors of great office buildings are not without evidence of courtship and its many allies.

Bundling has its evolution, and unless one is well versed in this lore, one fails to recognize some of our most modern courting arrangements as a part of the scheme of things first instituted in the ages long ago, and generally authorized by the well-known Naomi, mother-in-law of Ruth, who married Boaz after a novel bundling adventure.

(See the author's title on "Slants on the Origin of Bundling in the Old World.")

In the brochure now in your hand, we want to tell the story of bundling in the state of Pennsylvania, including, if space permits, occasional references to incidents elsewhere.

Is Bundling Wicked?—Naturally there will be two sides to the question, as to whether bundling, as a custom in the New World, is good, or bad.

Let us, for the moment, carry water on both shoulders—let us say that where the intent of young people to court in bed, is entirely honest, we subscribe to the theory that it cannot be morally wrong.

Under our present system of judging others by our own selfish ideas and longings, we do not anticipate that every bundling couple is going to violate the bounds of decency and morality.

It is a common human weakness to judge others by all the evil things we can conjure in our minds, to deprive others of what, deep down in our hearts we could relish with the greatest satisfaction (and which we secretly wish we could, perhaps, endure.)

It is the author's firm conviction, however, that gentlemen can be gentlemen at all times, and ladies can be ladies, as long as they want to, short of violence.

BUNDLING AN EXPEDIENT AMONG FRUGAL PEOPLE

Briefly, it Was an Expedient practiced among our people on a scarcity of beds, where, on occasion, husbands and parents frequently permitted travelers to bundle with their wives and daughters.

But this practice is world-wide, and always has been, in similar circumstances; particularly in some of the oriental countries not even approaching Christian in character—and where charity might otherwise be found wanting.

It was condoned in what we in America are prone to call "olden times," for the reason that young men, traveling far to see their sweethearts, could find better repose in bed, than to sit up all night; again, it did save fire-wood, which was not as scarce in colonial days as it has been lately! The saving of fire-wood was more of an excuse, than a necessity.

Bundling Was a Legitimate Custom, to all intents and purposes—with all its dangers—among most of the American colonists, in one way or another in those early days. Violations then, were not any greater than they would be today—except that today there seem to be easier ways to circumvent trouble.

The custom, happily for all concerned, was not confined alone to the courting couples, but was extended to army officers traveling from place to place, the good old peddler, and the traveling salesman; the minister and the doctor had the privilege, if they cared to exercise it; candidates for office could expect to be "invited" to join the family, or the daughter "in bed," if they had no fear as to some of the constituency raising objections as to "morals."

What may be legitimate to one person, may sound too-far-fetched for another. But it was great fun, yet to modest persons, sometimes quite a trial, when two or three and sometimes more old-fashioned families got to visit under one roof, and all went to bed together—or as many as could get in bed—others on the floor—some in the barn!

Nature requires that when one seeks rest at night, or even day, that sleeping persons should be fairly well covered; i. e., bed-clothing, or wraps of some kind should be provided to cover the body which, in slumber, becomes weak, and less-resistant to drafts.

So, in the course of time, wrapping up in several layers of bed-clothing came to be known as "bundling," or the equivalent of "tucking in," particularly of the youngsters, by the parents.

Whether the word "bundle" is English, or German in origin, we have never fully learned—but the idea back of it all is neither, in origin. It was but the natural evolution in the course of time.

It is nothing new to most of us—we know that two persons can keep warm in bed easier than one.

At best we can tell of certain phases of bundling but briefly. There is no point to the telling of it if we say it was found among the Germans in Pennsylvania only in colonial days; or that the Yankees practiced it, and had poems for and against the custom. Nor can we say, knowing all we do about the subject, that it died out, as the dictionary would have you believe, nearly a hundred years ago! As a matter of fact they probably have no knowledge of the evolution, and, at any rate, it would be unethical to speak too frankly about it here!

IS BUNDLING "BAD" FOR GIRLS, AND HARMLESS FOR BOYS?

Bundling Involves a Question of Morals.—Strange as it seems, the custom of bundling always seems to involve a question of morals—only of the female! Isn't it strange that no one seems to want to raise a question of morals as to whether or not it may be right and proper for a man to even "dare to sleep with a woman, to whom he is not married?"

It would seem to the author, and it ought to be rationally clear to the reader, too, that man is not so superior over woman that he might have the **right** to lie with her, or bundle with her, if he got a chance.

and yet, at the same time, declare it to be immoral for the girl to accept of his company? Can bundling be both right and wrong at one and the same time?

We have never yet seen a man who declared that he wouldn't accept the opportunity of bundling, either on the grounds that it might not be right, or that he might be "afraid" of the consequences — if he be honest.

On the other hand, we have met some females who doubt that they would indulge in this custom, while there are countless instances of some of the finest of wives and mothers today, who obtained fine husbands because they were not afraid to sleep with them single, and ended up morally and socially pure—and not prudes!

Naturally there are many homes, both rural and in the large centers of population, when large families are thrown together, and some not at all related;— compelled by force of circumstances to make the best of it at night as to sleeping accommodations.

It is difficult to form an opinion as to what harm comes from such commingling of young and old; boys and girls; men and women.

Actually, we doubt whether there is as much high license and immorality coming from such an experience, as there is with the boys and girls who have lived more or less alone, and have been starved in their learning about the laws of nature.

Brothers and sisters sleeping together as long as it is considered "safe" by parents, may or may not breed gentlemen and ladies.

Bundling as a whole is no more offensive today than in former times; mostly it is done in new and improvised and improved ways, due to the slow, but sure, elimination of the older customs from our more rural and suburban communities, where girls are still girls, and where boys know how to court; where coaxing may have little effect, and where parents know what transpires and keep their eye peeled, as compared with the city cousins who enjoy much of life, courting without the parents being even half-wise, or scarcely concerned.

MAGAZINE CONTRIBUTOR SAYS CUSTOM STILL PREVAILS

Bundling Still a Means to an End.—In an article in "The Mentor," for October, 1929, we read:

The practice of bundling is not yet dead in America, although you would have trouble finding it outside the few isolated counties that have been strong enough to resist the flow of creamy civilization with which we have been painted. We are assured that here and there in hinterland Pennsylvania the simple folk of German tradition still regard it as a means to an end. Doubtless it is to be found in forgotten townships of New England, where it had its greatest vogue in colonial days. It is said to survive in vestige form in Wisconsin and Minnesota and, far from generally, it is practiced today in the mountains of Kentucky, W. Virginia, Tennessee and North Carolina. And before we go further it must be clearly understood that bundling has nothing to do nor anything in common with the casual promiscuity of the simple negro. Bundling was a custom, not a convenience.*

Bundling was practiced in two forms, and while the first was a bit startling to the uninitiated the second had economic recommendations which alone placed it above the status of its degenerate offspring—"keeping company." Moreover, it was a custom imported into America and not indigenous to the colonies. It came west with the Welsh, the English, the Holland Dutch, the Germans, and even the Calvinistic Scotch. The make-shift social conditions in the colonies were responsible for its high favor and development here.

There were districts in New England where the bundling light was a beacon to the farm lad who, of a Saturday night, went trudging afoot or on horse up the roads invoking and even daring fate. The Yankee with daughters to wed advertised the fact in this poetic manner. He had merely to put a candle in his window (more often it was the mother who lighted it or the marriageable girl herself) and bide the family's time.

That fate might not find her unreceptive, the daughter thus offered for mating enjoyed the distinction of a room of her

---

*While we can agree with the "Mentor" article in general, we believe we have a right to differ on the conclusion that bundling was a "custom" only, and not a "convenience." It seems logical to assume that it was difficult to differentiate between the two. In fact, all the publicity of other years seems to have excused the "custom" on the grounds of economic "necessity," when it probably was truly a "convenience" which permitted of frugality at the same time.—Ed.

own and a bed of feathers. To this she was wont to retire early . . .
Presently the knight-errant, seeing the light, halted in his quest and tapped briskly on the pane . . .
Even if his features were more or less obscure through the window pane, yet he was a male and as such he was to be permitted to enter (through the window) for better or for worse. The bundling set in almost instantly, as verbal fencings and soft blandishments did not flourish in the early American farm house . . . Talking was not a fine art and therefore disregarded by the wise . . .

BUNDLING IN THE NEW ENGLAND STATES

New England.—In the early history of the colonies New England particularly was faced with some disaccommodations due to the barrenness of that part of the country. They had to be ingenious, but that did not prevent them from practicing some customs they acquired in their sojourn in England and Holland before that.

Therefore we are not at all surprised to find among the Yankees the first active evidences of "bundling," "tarrying," and later perhaps in New York, of the custom known as "queesting."

Diedrich Knickerbocker told some very interesting accounts of these early bundlers, but in the cold, clear light of modern understanding, the earlier settlers must have contributed quite a bit to bundling lore, which has since been lost to us through generations of increasing wealth and of larger homes.

There was a sort of war, or at least conflict between certain classes and favorites for, and those against the custom, and there issued at times, next to scorching poems on the subject.

One reason for the Yankee abhorrance that once existed, may be indicated in a portion of the "History of New York," by Washington Irving, (D.K.) wherein he says:

To this sagacious custom, therefore, do I chiefly attribute the unparalleled increase of the Yanokie or Yankee tribe; for it is a certain fact, well authenticated by court records and parish registers, that wherever the practice of bundling prevailed, there was an amazing number of sturdy brats annually born unto the state. without the license of the law, or the benefit of clergy . . .

Of Connecticut, we hear Rev. Samuel Peter's speak, saying:

The women of Connecticut are strictly virtuous, and to be compared to the prude rather that the European polite lady . . . Notwithstanding the modesty of the females is such that it would be accounted the greatest rudeness for a gentleman to speak before a lady of a garter, knee, or leg, yet it is thought but a piece of civility to ask her to bundle; a custom as old as the first settlement of 1634. It is certainly innocent, virtuous and prudent, or the puritans would not have permitted it to prevail among their offspring, for whom in general they would have suffered crucifixion . . . I am no advocate for temptation; yet must say, that bundling has prevailed 160 years in New England, and, I verily believe, with **ten times more chastity than sitting on a sofa** . . . **The sofa is more dangerous in summer, than the bed in winter** . . .

The story is told of a damsel in Connecticut, who expected her lover to come and bundle with her, that her mother bade her put both her legs into a pillowcase, and tie it around her waist. The next morning mother asked her if she kept her "limbs" in the bag, to which the innocent Miss replied, "Ma, dear, I only took one out!"

A general concensus of opinion of fathers in New England, seemed to bear out the theory that there was less of bungling in the days of bundling, than in later years. Quite often we read of such conclusions. Bundling is, after all, a matter of continence— a matter of intent, or purpose—

PENNSYLVANIA OFFERS PLENTY OF EVIDENCE

Many Different Methods Used.—Among the many accounts relative to bundling in Pennsylvania is that of Stiles' reference to the old schoolmaster of Glastonbury, Conn., about the 1850's, who told of his experiences in teaching in the southern part of the state, and speaking of boarding around. From the nature of the account we believe it to be more in the form of flippantry, than an evidence of the practice.

There is plenty of evidence here — both past and present, parts of which we give you as these accounts came to us from either those who told it to us, or from authentic works containing references.

In the author's larger and more inclusive work, he enumerates and shows the evolution of bundling from early days in America down to date. Herein it is his purpose to collate some specific instances wherein bundling has taken place in Pennsylvania—in spite of the fact that several judges, and a number of others more or less in the public eye, have held that it probably never existed, or perhaps only in our imagination.

Actually, we suppose they doubt its prevalence in the Keystone State, because they had never indulged in the practice, or felt ashamed thereof.

"Bundle" Expressions have been reported in many different ways in Pennsylvania, among them being: "Bundle up before you go out, or before you go to school;" "I'll bundle you right off to bed." Before anti-freeze was used in autos, we "bundled the radiator" of the car, same as we used to do the faithful horse.

For a girl to have "bungled" when bundling, we say in Pennsylvania-German: "Se iss ufgabundled!"

Original Methods for bundling in these parts were the same as in New England, where they either bundled with their clothes on, or made some slight attempts at going to bed with some clothing discarded, prepared to rest.

Our people are so ill-prepared to picture the colonial home and its contents, that they cannot get a clear picture of what some folks had to go through every day of their lives; and their nights were little or no better than their days.

Suppose we take the account of Dr. A., of Ligonier, who tells us of a typical back-woods hut in which we "make out" that there must have been some bundling, to say the least, if the place wasn't otherwise overcrowded! Read this carefully, for there is a great deal jammed into a small room. The doctor said:

"A family of 11 children, the parents, and two

aunts; one child died. Three girls married, bringing their husbands home to live. Two became mothers, and their mother, a mother again;—thus, 3 babies in two years' time." All were attended by Dr. A. Total in house, 20.

Size of bed-room, containing three beds, one bureau, a wash-stand, fire-place and one window which could not be opened—about 10x14 feet! The living room was scarcely any larger; the chimney was placed in the center. A small bed, perhaps trundle, had to be stepped on to get to the bureau.

The girls were married at around fifteen years of age, and, it appears they had some useful and perhaps guilty knowledge before they brought their husbands home. Where, and how 20 people could actually sleep in that home will puzzle most readers.

The before-mentioned family was the same, we believe, as that one from which came a young man who went to the University of Pennsylvania Medical School, and from which he graduated with the highest marks ever attained by a medical student in that institution (about 1880).

So much for an instance which, to our way of thinking, furnishes an excellent location for bundling.

EARLY SETTLERS DEVISE METHODS TO SUIT CONVENIENCE

Our Early Settlers German.—Pennsylvania is largely settled by Swiss or Germanic people—generally of substantial families—many of them of the bundling type. It has been evident throughout the history of this state that neither the Germans, nor their customs, no matter how odd, or peculiar, or how liberal, have hurt the home, church, or industrial life of the state a single iota. In fact their ways of living have done much to keep the state in the forefront as a real accomplishment in the nation.

Thad. Stevens stated that for every case of bundling in Lancaster county, there were twenty cases in Vermont! Poor Thad.; we doubt whether he made much of an investigation before he made the statement.

It has been not so long since that fellows bundled in bed with their girls in Dauphin, substantially a suburb of Harrisburg.

Another tells us that he bundled in Schuylkill county, not so long ago. We have even determined that a young lady of twenty-two years, learned of bundling in her high school course in social sciences about the year 1933, in this same locality.

The section around the junction points of Northumberland, Dauphin and Schuylkill counties is said to be a fine region for bundling, even today.

Another says: "When I was a boy in Mifflin county, I was told they bundled in Snyder county." The same person admitted that there probably was a great amount of it in Mifflin county, too, for where there are Amish people, there is bundling. Mifflin county also has a healthy number of Penna.-German rural population, and the author knows these people well enough to state positively that the central section of the state finds any amount of bundling, both in bed, and on the davenport—not to speak of the automobile.

A Mennonite college professor tells that among his people there is no little bundling, although we note that one of the bishops for them, in the state of Indiana, says it is not so. Oh, well; we always did hold to the theory that not everyone knew everything; perhaps the bishop just didn't know. Besides, there are substantially ten dozen different kinds of Mennonites, and it may be, after all, that his group is better than those in Pennsylvania, and Canada, though we doubt it—in fact we deny it!

The Amish of Big Valley, Mifflin county, are regular bundlers; and we hope those of Lancaster, too. These are said to court with the sheet between the couple—britches having taken their flight, if so disposed. There is no room in an Amishman's home in which a couple could court, except the kitchen, and a bench, or chair, or perhaps the wood-box, offer the only place on which to rest, unless on the kitchen-table, or the floor. Between these, and a bed—we'd take the bed, and we believe every other sensible person would do likewise.

Typical old-fashioned bed and bed-room; ideal for "bundling."

CONCLUSIVE EVIDENCE OF BUNDLING AMONG THE "PLAIN PEOPLE"

Courting in Bed, and Sitting Upright.—The author has been accused from time to time, of drawing from his imagination on the matter of "bundling" among the "plain people" (which was not in accord with the facts, and with credit where credit is due.)

Now we are in position to quote additionally from an official organ of the Amish Mennonite Churches, (Old Order and Conservative), entitled "Herold der Wahrheit," ("Herald of Truth").

In several brief instalments in the "Herold" in the January and February issues, for 1937, the matter of "bundling" is discussed by one who would even go so far as to tell the bishops, and ministers, that the old custom is "wrong," even if they personally indulged in it in their youth—and by their indifference (or sense of caution) still encourage it today.

Traditionally we suppose that bundling in bed would be about the extent of "prohibition" suggested by a laymen, but see to what lengths this writer takes us: "Today it seems to be the most popular practice among the young sisters of our Amish Mennonite churches to disregard, remove, and lay aside the devotional head covering during courting hours. WHY?

"Of course we all know that it is wrong for a woman to pray with her head uncovered. But, you may ask, why would it be wrong for her to 'entertain' her boy friend with her head uncovered? Perhaps you will say you neither pray nor prophesy when he is there. If that is the case—**young brother, you'd be safer at home.**"

It is common knowledge, or should be, that the women-folk of the "plain people" keep their heads covered at all times, being then in readiness to pray points out that "human flesh cannot be trusted."

He speaks of the "bitter agony suffered by the fallen sister who has spent whole nights in weeping and mourning because she has lost the honorable and sacred blessedness of virgin purity, never to find it again . . ." Had she kept her covering on her head some of these mis-steps might not have occurred. How she lost her virgin purity we fail to understand, unless he means it in the light of their reasoning that "virgin" means good also spiritually and in thoughts, as is common among them.

The article continues: "During those courting hours time is not all taken up in conversation . . . What are we thinking of during those silent moments? . . . When we forget to even think of God; to consider whether He is pleased or grieved; yea, when courtship (?) is indulged just for **silly fun;** and when we trust our own strength against the craftiness of the devil, those silent moments may be **dangerous.** For a child of God, who engages in courtship, it is very essential and necessary to pray . . . " hence the need to wear the head covering!

"If the way, in which many (yea, alas! too many!) courtships among us Amish young people are conducted, were made known to the public! . . . There are those of other denominations who highly esteemed and respected the Amish Church, but when they learned of our, we must admit, low-down standard of courtship they were utterly shocked . . ." indicating that others practicing this old custom did not always profess themselves to be Christians—and that other Christian denominations did not practice it!

"In the first place," he continues, "it is greatly to be feared that a large percentage of the popularly so-called 'dates' among us Amish young people of today, are only 'dates' and no real courtship whatsoever. Is it not sadly true that of many, many 'dates' the motive is not honest, true, sincere, pure and careful Christian love? But it is really done more because of a desire and a craving for an unholy lustly 'necking' (as it has been termed by many and rightly so). This is an ungodly motive . . .

"Where is there a **modest** brother or sister who could without shame confess the practice of bed courtship? This term includes not only 'under the cover' but on top of the cover as well . . .

Bundling in the New World 19

"Why is bed courtship wrong? . . . Any one with ordinary mental ability very well knows that the Devotional Covering and bed courtship do not go well together . . . The Covering denotes (or at least it should) modesty, respect, chastity, purity, subjection, and obedience; while bed courtship readily indicates immodesty, immorality, unchasteness, carelessness, impudence, indecency, shamelessness, lack of respect for one another, and lack of self-respect."

The brother of some mis-givings and fears, says: "Of course we know and realize that our opponents on this subject are not all young folks and lay members, but we frankly admit, and this with some shame, that there are even some ministers and bishops among our denomination who seek to justify this. Some say, 'Es is der alt Gebrauch:' and, 'Es is die alt Ordnung.' . . ." (meaning "it is the old need, or order.")

The writer then continues: "It has also been said in regard to courting in a sitting position, 'Es fiihrt in der Hochmuth' (it leads to pride) . . . The commonly approved type of courtship may be equal with that of the world; but bundling is lower than that . . ."

"Because bed courtship is different by no means makes it better, more respectable, more modest, or more pleasing to God . . ."

Our contemporary is human in the light of his reasoning when he says: "When we were little boys and girls, and as we entered the early teen-age we used to wonder how the young folks conducted courtship . . . that when we learned of bed courtship, we were greatly shocked . . . How did we (the writer included) ever get to the point that we became guilty of this practice? . . ." and to which your author raises another question.

Can children or young folks raise any question as to the propriety of bed courtship, or "bundling," unless they already have a guilty knowledge?

The Amish writer quotes many references in the Bible to support his reasonings, but fails to quote from the interesting account of Ruth and Boaz, in Ruth iii, verses 6 and 13!

AUTHOR'S FRIEND NEARLY LOSES TROUSERS

It Must Not be Forgotten that the author is a native of Snyder county, and being honest to a fault, admits that evidences of bundling were present during his boyhood days—and still remain.

A fellow (friend of the author), couldn't go calling on the same girl for ten years or longer, nearly always retiring with her on the davenport, after taking off his coat, vest and trousers, without becoming an inveterate bundler! Taking off the whole suit, as he usually did, was to him what saving fire-wood was to the Yankee, or Welshman—a good excuse; it saved pressing the suit after it would have been wrinkled a-plenty.

Trousers as worn by the poorer sort of country boys, would not stand wearing and sleeping-in for 24 hours a day; they rarely ever get a pressing iron.

Once a young man got his long trousers, or even his short pants or knicker suits for that matter—they never saw a pressing iron—the suit was worn for good until it was worn too much for good; then it gave way to a new suit, and so on. While it was natural to be careful with clothing—and he had to be presentable so that his pants and coat would be kept in good condition—if he courted this same girl for a decade, he must have been careful with his bundling, too.

The individual we have in mind told us that on one occasion on a Sunday morning the dog dragged his trousers out of the room, and he couldn't find them when the girl's father came down to do the chores around the barn.

We inquired what the father had to say when he caught him with his pants off, and he related that nothing was said, and the girl was not annoyed at the predicament—which, apparently, was not a predicament after all. After a number of years a prospective father-in-law ought to trust a fellow, don't you think?

Intemperance in bundling is like intemperance in anything else; the abusers and violators pay the bill.

ANOTHER AUTHENTIC ACCOUNT OF THE CENTER-BOARD

The Center-Board Again.—An old friend of the writer's family, now resident in Altoona, tells one on himself. He was a telegraph operator, near Lewistown, on the Sunbury and Lewistown division of the Pennsylvania railroad, soon after the opening of the line in the 1870's. He was invited, after some acquaintance, to spend the night with a Dunker girl a few miles away. So he packed his night-shirt and went to make the call.

He told how, after a short visit in the early hours of the evening, he was ushered to his bed-room by one of the adult members of the family. On getting ready for bed he was surprised when his "date" came into his room, and he suspended his undressing operations for the moment. He inquired whether she wasn't going to get to bed (assuming she had her own room), when she replied that she would sleep with him. He said at the time he hardly knew how to act—that he had believed the girl up to that time to be a model of innocence, sincerity, and perfection.

But he resumed his preparations for bed, and she followed him directly to the place where sweet repose ought to find all of us.

She told him, when he asked her whether it was proper for her to be in bed with him, that it was a custom among her people to allow the young folks certain privileges; that she trusted him in everything, and that he need have no fear to be with her, even in bed!

He said that all he did that night was talk until about two o'clock, when he dropped off to sleep.

As it is recalled, they were separated by a single sheet, plus the night-clothing they wore. During the conversation, we recalled to him that sometimes center-boards were used to keep the lovers apart, and he again remembered that the bed in which he slept on the night in question, had a recessed place, head and foot ends, reasons for which he inquired from her.

The young lady told him that formerly her people erected a barrier which consisted of a wide board, running the full length of the bed, over which, she told, none ventured far, except in fear of being beaten up by members of the family who would respond at the least sign of trouble. "Honest men and women can lay quiet all the night!"

Pillows, Bolsters, Bags.—In addition to the centerboard there were other obstacles, more or less, in the middle of the bed. One of these was the long pillow, or bolster. These were as effective as the sword which somewhere in history was indicated as a warning against "trespassing."

Bundling bags were not unusual, though it is difficult these days to find persons who go to such lengths to make themselves uncomfortably safe. Our liberality of thought allows us more latitude and longitude in our courting, and if men and women are honest, they still can lay quiet all the night!

Dictionary Outmoded?—A Schuylkill county judge tells us that he met a married man in Lehigh county in 1872, who told him that bundling had been the custom in that part of the county where he had lived when a young man, but that it had gone out of practice since. He feels that we have overdrawn the presence of bundling in this state, claiming that the largest dictionaries always ascribe it to New England and Wales.

But the judge must remember that the dictionaries he refers to were published before our findings were made available. If we make the statement that we will try to have the dictionaries amended, will it sound like an idle boast? At least we can try!

Bundling Is a Test.—Girls are usually as willing, if not more so, to bundle, than men; for they know just about what they want to do, or how far they dare go—while men usually crawl into bed hesitatingly, with doubts, and misgivings, as to the arrangement—whether, perhaps, something untoward might not happen after all. This is a probationary test—whether by ritual, or custom, or experiment.

WHERE COURTING REALLY IS SOMETHING REAL!

Bundling Par Excellence.—There are other tests coming under the term bundling, in widely scattered portions of the world. But there is one community in Pennsylvania (and several like it elsewhere in America), where bundling is merely a passing incident in the matter of courtship. It is declared with emphasis, and based on facts, that a large number of young men courted and loved their girls so intensely that they went to the extreme beyond that of bundling, in their test of the girls, for they, coming to be farmers in but a few years, did not want to marry girls incapable of becoming mothers. So the rule was applied to "show me first, and I'll marry you afterward."

No legal, moral or social difficulties seem to have beset these people at any time because of, what to the average person would seem rather the extreme.

In that section of our state wherein this custom once was largely practiced, the persons indulging in this practice had nothing in common with the similar practice in Wales—except the resulting progeny.

Marriages in royal families appear to be based on a similar basis, yet to the person not at all concerned in practices of this kind it appears rather daring.

We can say here, in passing, that bundling was also practiced in Scotland, England and Wales in particular, most frequently in no uncertain fashion.

We wish we had space to spare, and could excerpt enough from our previous books on bundling, and others, on English social conditions, to give the reader something along the line not as self-controlled as that of bundling between the lovers.

Improvised For the Moment.—A good friend informs us that bundling persisted in Allegheny county, among the Scotch-Irish, evidently as late as the 1870's. Perhaps he didn't know the evolution of this custom, or he could tell of countless cases where it still exists in the same county.

He also tells of an emergency about the year 1930,

in Pittsburgh, N. S., where a young lady, alone at night at the locked door of friends whom she expected to return (but who didn't)—accepted the invitation, in good faith, to spend the night with a charitable neighbor—a young gentleman.

The young man was not necessarily pleasure-bent (as most of us would under similar circumstances), and when she inquired, on retiring, for a needle and thread, he was rather surprised to note later on, as the young lady was crawling into bed, that she had sewed her slip from hem up, between her legs, far enough to provide an excellent pair of pajamas for the occasion. Just another evidence of necessity being the mother of invention—or convention!

We find in checking over the court records in this state that apparently only one case of bundling was important enough to reach the courts. It was that of Hollis v. Wells, August Term, 1845, in the Court of Common Pleas of Lehigh County (see Law reports; or "Bundling Prohibited!" published by the Aurand Press, Harrisburg, Pa., 1929).

SOME SCATTERED REFERENCES TO BUNDLING IN AMERICA

Bundling Still a Custom.—Skeptics need not look far for evidences of bundling today. A widely circulated magazine late in 1937 published a picture of a married couple in their bed, separated by a heavy plank, through which had been driven twenty-penny spikes, **toward the side occupied by the wife.** She went to court, and got her divorce on the grounds of cruelty. It appears one of the first instances of the kind, where the male erected a "bundling" barrier to keep the female strictly on her side of the "fence."

Early in 1938, a man in Camden, N. J., obtained his divorce on the grounds that for ten years he was compelled to sleep with his wife with a "pillow, or bolster" between them. Each had their own set of bed clothes. Someone says that this case represented one of the most pathetic he had ever seen.

Those of us who read the newspapers more or less

Bundling in the New World 25

at length, note the frequent murders of lovers, young and old, in isolated places, such as the woods, in lonely country lanes, along the lakes and rivers, or in tourist cabins; even in private apartments and homes. Many of these murders are unsolved. If young persons are honest, and sincere, would it not be a lot nicer, and a great deal safer, to conduct their love-affairs right in the girl's own home—if she is fortunate enough to have one—than too much in the open?

Even hard-hearted land-ladies might be willing to allow more courting in their homes and flats, if they could be persuaded that forcing decent, and innocent young women to go elsewhere for the purpose of companionship and love, quite often contributes to the down-fall of those who would be good, if they were not compelled to be as we say, "bad."

Bundling signals to swains included not only the lighted candle at the window, or perhaps two of them, but the arrangement of window shades, and many other devices too numerous to mention. Some of these signals later on became the common signal in the red-light districts—(or is it the other way 'round?)

Women of shady reputation generally use a blind arrangement, or certain colored lights, as the informed well know. But is it true that the Amish of Lancaster county use "blue gates" for the purpose of advertising that there lives within that home a "virgin" ready for the marriage block? Hardly. (See "Little Known Facts About the Amish and the Mennonites," by the author of "Little Known Facts About Bundling.")

It must be remembered that few travelers get into the rural sections where we would naturally expect to find the custom still in practice. Bundling is not advertised to the public like the farmers advertise that they have for sale "apples, corn, eggs, ham and other products of the farm."

The Peddlers and Salesmen of a generation ago, cannot bring to us the wealth of lore once common to our system of news dissemination. But bundling did not pass away with the salesmen—we still have the lovers who practice it as it pleases them—and they do not need a book of this kind to indicate to them that it was, and still is, and probably will be for a long time, a convenient way for them to court —even by lying in bed—if they can be honest! Bundling has advantages and disadvantages. It is a convenient way to keep girls at home, and practical, too. Accidents here, like with automobiles, do not happen—they are caused; and with about the same kind of "drivers and passengers."

The places where bundling may occur, pretty-well run the length of the dictionary, and we need not repeat that they include almost any place where men and women can recline at all. Yet we have read of accounts of bundling occurring in out-door toilets in certain sections of the British Isles, and in Wales particularly. The poor have little choice in the matter of love and courtship.

Indian maidens in Western America wound ropes around their legs during courtship affairs. This is but another one of many ways that courting was made safe, by some obstacle being placed between lovers.

The information came unsolicited some time ago, that a Harrisburg man bundled in Troy, Pa., in the year 1914—said episode occurring with a girl in a bag! Believe it to be the truth—we do.

Col. Henry W. Shoemaker, of McElhattan, reports the accession of a bed with a center-board.

Whatever you want to call it—bundling, courting in bed, queesting, tarrying, sparkin', splitting the bed, or a thousand and one other terms—let us be fair. Suppose for a moment that you, the reader, were morally honest, and wanted to live according to the christian and social standards of the day—where do you think you would be safest from falling into evil ways? In bed—where others can hear your voice if raised in fear, or doubt? In the barn; or the hay-mow? In the wood-shed? In the woods? In the auto, miles from home, and off the public highway? In a cabin in the mountains, or a cottage by the sea?

Again we ask—isn't a virgin girl, or an honest one at least, better off at home in bed with her lover— with all the temptation that may befall—than in the barn, or woods, or park, or miles away in an auto?

THE CANDIDATE AND MAID WHO DIDN'T GET TO BUNDLE

One of Those "Pathetic Stories."—They tell this story pretty well over the entire state of Pennsylvania.

It is about a candidate for sheriff, some years ago. The office-seeker came to a rural home late in the afternoon. He inquired whether he could obtain a meal, and lodging for the night. The reply was that he could have both. The supper was a fine one, and the candidate was in fine humor.

As was customary in those days, folks went to bed rather early, and on announcing that he believed he would be off to bed, if they would tell him where to sleep, he'd retire.

The farmer said "We don't have much room, but you can sleep with the hired girl."

The candidate replied that he was a married man, and a candidate, too, and that if it became generally known throughout the county that he had slept with a hired girl during his campaign, that some constituents might misconstrue his motives and manners; could he have no other place to sleep? The farmer said the only other place he could think of was in the barn.

So rather than chance it to sleep with the hired girl on account of what might have happened to him, and his campaign, he decided on the barn.

Early next morning he heard the hired girl come into the cow stable to let out the cows.

After milking one or two, she came back to release a bull which had become restless, leading him to one of the cows. The story goes that the bull sniffed around a bit, turning his head, and drawing away.

This infuriated the maid, and she yelled at the bull in evident disgust: "What the devil's a-matter with you? Are you a candidate for sheriff too?"

THE POETS SHOW A HAND IN THE GAME OF BUNDLING

There is hardly a subject under the sun that poets do not touch with their hand. Preserved in old almanacs and some books on the subject, we find occasional selections. Some of them are quite entertaining, one of which we give you here, entitled:

A NEW SONG IN FAVOR OF COURTING
(Known also as "The Whore on the Snow Crust.")

Adam at first was formed of dust,
As we find of record;
And did receive a wife call'd Eve,
By a creative word.

From Adam's side a crooked bride,
We find complete in form;
Ordained that they in bed might lay
And keep each other warm.

To court indeed they had no need,
She was his wife at first,
And she was made to be his aid,
Whose origin was dust.

This new made pair full happy were,
And happy might remained,
If his help meet had never eat
The fruit that was restrained.

Tho' Adam's wife destroyed his life
In manner that is awfull;
Yet marriage now we all allow
[To] Be both just and lawfull.

And now a days there is two ways,
Which of the two is right
To lie between sheets sweet and clean
Or sit up all the night.

But some suppose bundling in clothes
The good and wise doth vex;
Then let me know which way to go
To court the fairer sex.

Whether they must be hug'd and bus'd
When setting up all night;
Or whether [they] in bed may lay,
Which doth reason invite?

Nature's request is, give me rest,
Our bodies seek repose;
Night is the time, and 'tis no crime
To bundle in our cloaths.

Since in a bed, a man and maid
May bundle and be chaste:
It doth no good to burn up wood;
It is a needless waste.

Let coat and shift be turned
    adrift,
And breeches take their
    flight,
An honest man and virgin
    can
Lie quiet all the night.
But if there be dishonesty
    Implanted in the mind,
Breeches nor smocks, nor
    scarce padlocks
The rage of lust can bind.
Cate, Nance and Sue proved
    just and true,
Tho' bundling did practise;
But Ruth beguil'd and proved
    with child,
Who bundling did despise.
Whores will be whores, and
    on the floor
Where many has been laid,
To set and smoke and ashes
    poke,
Wont keep awake a maid.
Bastards are not at all times
    got
In feather beds we know;
The strumpet's oath convin-
    ces both
Oft times it is not so.
One whorish dame, I fear to
    name
Lest I should give offence,
But in this town she was took
    down
Not more than eight
    months since.
She was the first, that on
    snow crust,
I ever knew to gender;
I'll hint no more about this
    whore
For fear I should offend
    her.
'Twas on the snow when Sol
    was low,
And was in Capricorn,
A child was got, and it will
    not
Be long ere it is born.

Now unto those that do op-
    pose
The bundling traid, I say
Perhaps there's more got on
    the floor,
Than any other way.
In ancient books no know-
    ledge is
Of these things to be got;
Whether young men did
    bundle then,
Or whether they did not.
Sence ancient book says wife
    they took,
It don't say how they
    courted;
Whether young men did
    bundle then,
Or by the fire sported.
[But some do hold in times
    of old,
That those about to wed,
Spent not the night, nor yet
    the light,
By fire, or in the bed.]
They only meant to say they
    sent
A man to choose a bride:
Isaac was so, but let me
    know,
If any one beside.
Men don't pretend to trust a
    friend
To choose him sheep or
    cows;
Much more a wife whom all
    his life
He does except to house.
Sense it doth stand each one
    in hand
To happify his life;
I would advise each to be
    wise,
And choose a prudent wife.
Sense bundling is not a thing
That judgment will pro-
    cure;
Go on young men and bun-
    dle then,
But keep your bodies pure.

But where we have persons in favor of this or that, we also find some opposed, and this was true in the matter of bundling. The following is said to have been written by a learned and distinguished clergyman settled in Bristol county, Mass., who was a graduate of Harvard University, and a doctor of divinity.

A POEM AGAINST BUNDLING
(Dedicated to Ye Youth of Both Sexes.)

Hail giddy youth, inclined to mirth,
To guilty amours prone,
Come blush with me, to think and see
How shameless you are grown.

'Tis not amiss to court and kiss,
Nor friendship do we blame,
But bundling in, women with men,
Upon the bed of shame;

And there to lay till break of day,
And think it is no sin,
Because a smock and petticoat
Have chanced to lie between.

Such rank disgrace and scandal base,
All modest youth will shun,
For 'twill infest, like plague or pest,
And you will be undone.

Let boars and swine lie down and twine,
And grunt, and, sleep, and snore,
But modest girls should not wear tails
Nor bristles any more.

Let rams the sheep mount up and leap,
Without restraint or blame,

But will young men act just like them?
Oh, 'tis a burning shame!

It is not strange that horses range
Unfettered to the last,
But youthful lusts in fetters must
Be chained to virtue fast.

Dogs and bitches wear no breeches,
Clothing for man was made,
Yet men and women strip to their linen,
And tumble into bed.

Yes, brutal youth, it is the truth,
Your modesty is gone,
And could you blush, you'd think as much,
And curse what you have done.

To have done so some years ago,
Was counted more disgrace
Than 'tis of late to propagate
A spurious bastard race.

Quit human kind and herd with swine,
Confess yourself an whore;
Go fill the stye, there live and die,
Or bundle never more.

Shall gentlemen with ladies join
To practice like the brutes,

Bundling in the New World 31

Then let them keep with cattle and sheep,
And fodder on their fruits.
This cursed course is one great source
Of matches undesigned,
Quarrels and strife twixt man and wife,
And bastards of their kind.
But in excuse of this abuse
It oftentimes is said,
Father and mother did no other
Than strip and go to bed.
But grant some did as you have said,
Yet do they not repent,
And wish that you may never do
What they so much lament?
A stupid ass can't be more base,
Than are those guilty youth
Who fill with smart a parent's heart,
And turn it into mirth.
Others do plead hard for the bed,
Their health and weariness,
So drunkards will drink down their swill,
And call it no excess.
Under pretense of self-defense,
Others will scold and say,
An honest maid is chaste abed
As any other way.
But where's the man that fire can
Into his bosom take,
Or go through coals on his foot soles
And not a blister make?
Temptation's way has led astray
The likeliest of you all,
And yet you're found on slippery ground,
And think you cannot fall.
A female meek, with blushing cheek,
Seized in some lover's arms,
Has oft grown weak with Cupid's heat
And lost her virgin charms.
But last of all, up speaks romp Moll
And pleads to be excused,
For how can she e'er married be
If bundling be refused?
What strange mistake young women,
To hope for sparks this way!
Your fond bold acts can't lay a tax
That men will ever pay!
So cheap and free some women be,
That men are cloyed with sweet,
As horse or cow starve at the mow
With fodder under feet.
'Tis therefore vain yourselves to screen,
The practice is accurst,
It is condemned by God and man,
The pious and the just.
Should you go on, the day will come,
When Christ your judge will say,
In "bundles" bind each of this kind,
And cast them all away.
Down deep in hell there let them dwell,
And bundle on that bed;
There burn and roll without control,
'Till all their lusts are fed.

Just in case your don't know; left to right: a cotton petticoat; pair cotton stockings, and a pair of drawers, or "pants," as formerly known. Pants were worn by women in all walks of life only a few years ago! These represent a middle grade, compared with the long, tight "duck material" variety worn by many of the "plain people," and the more delicate fabrics of our day. Even the dog seems just a little bit interested in our story!

www.ingramcontent.com/pod-product-compliance
Lightning Source LLC
Chambersburg PA
CBHW031439040426
42444CB00006B/895